The Heart Room

poems by

Libby Kurz

Finishing Line Press
Georgetown, Kentucky

The Heart Room

For Chris

The line of words fingers your own heart. It invades arteries, and enters the heart on a flood of breath; it presses the moving rims of thick valves; it palpates the dark muscle strong as horses, feeling for something, it knows not what.

Annie Dillard

ACKNOWLEDGMENTS

These poems were first published in the following journals, to whose editors
grateful acknowledgement is made:

"Compressions" published in issue 44 of *Ruminate*
"Distance" published in issue 4.1 of *Driftwood Press*
"The Meaning of Life" and "March" published in the Spring 2016 issue of
Relief Journal
"Fall" and "Negligence" published in *Mothers Always Write*

***

Thank you to the Poetry Society of Virginia for awarding prizes to the
following poems:
"How to Handle a Heart" – First place in the 2017 New Voices category
"Transplant" – Second place in the 2017 Charlotte Wise Memorial category

Publisher: Leah Maines
Editor: Christen Kincaid
Cover Art: Aaron McCall
Author Photo: Brianna Card, Bree Card Photography
Cover Design: Leah Huete

Printed in the USA on acid-free paper.
Order online: www.finishinglinepress.com
             also available on amazon.com

Author inquiries and mail orders:
Finishing Line Press
P. O. Box 1626
Georgetown, Kentucky 40324
U. S. A.

Table of Contents

How to Handle a Heart...1

Negative Space 3

Newlywed 5

Time of Death 6

Hands...8

Convergence...10

Mild..12

Part of Me 13

Anniversary...14

Compressions...15

Pursuit..17

Distance 18

Absence..19

Midlife..20

The Meaning of Life 21

Fall 23

Transplant..24

Cold Hope 26

Sustenance 28

March 30

Negligence 32

Note to Self...34

Exhale...35

How to Handle a Heart

Wear gloves tightly
fitted to your fingers,
but not too tight—

you will want to feel
the surface purely,

the way the vessels
hug the muscle
like roots that shoot
deep into the damp
body of the earth.

You will want to feel
the tissue pulsing
because it's like
listening to music
in your hand,

and it will make you think
that maybe the day
God created
the human heart
was the same day
He made rhythm
and set the entire planet
to one beat,

and when you're done
you must shake it briskly—

let any air out
that might be trapped
inside the chambers—
but not too hard, because
it's like cupping a bird
in your hands—

the one that got stuck
in your house
through an open window,

the one you've managed
to coax and capture,

the one whose hollow body
you feel flailing inside your palm
as you walk onto the front lawn,
release your gap-toothed grip

and watch its wings
spread widely
into the open sky,
pumping the air
like blood.

Negative Space

Each morning during first period
I sat in the art studio
and watched my boyfriend
pass by, walking from the parking lot
down to the main building.

The windows were made of ice cube glass,
so his form was blurry, but I knew
the shape of his body, the way it moved,
the colors of his high school jacket.

Sometimes he waved,
sometimes he gave a faint nod,
trying to be cool in front of his friends.

Sometimes, if he was mad at me,
he wouldn't look at me at all,
or he'd look at me with no gesture.

That's what really killed me—the recognition
without a recognition,

the way I could see through the glass
but only a vague image.

Womanhood was coming for me—
my arm pits sweating, the rest of me shivering,
my body teaching me how to house
both positive and negative space,

like the drawings I would start in the
dark room with the overhead projector,
enlarging a face to the desired size
so I could trace the outline.

Free hand drawing was never my strength.
I wanted to spend my time not on the shape,
but inside of the shape:

the shades and shadows,
the slopes and fissures,
the way the light would hit a thing
and leave darkness on the other side.

Newlywed

I'm drinking a cup of coffee
from our Café Du Monde mug.

Do you remember the first time
we went there, seven years ago,

just engaged? We sat in the shade
of the striped tent, powdered sugar

on your unshaven face
as we ate airy beignets

and sipped chicory coffee
so dark we could see our reflections

on the surface. We were ignorant
of the innocence of the French Quarter

before Katrina—ten months shy
of when the big storm hit.

That first year of marriage—
learning how to fight, how to let go,

how to ride the tumultuous tides
we don't mean to trigger in one another,

how to stand still on a slanted rooftop,
waiting to be saved, because we are

too in love with our own city
to help ourselves.

Time of Death

No one prepared me
for the details in real time—

the way human eyes widen
and stare off so blankly
at one fixed point
it is impossible to decipher
whether they are looking
inward or outward or
nowhere at all,

or the way the tongue
protrudes from the mouth,
swollen around the breathing tube
as if to say, *Enough.*

They forgot to mention
how it would feel to walk
into a hospital supply room
at 4am on a Sunday morning
to grab a morgue bag
from the metal utility shelf,
to carry it back into
the operating room
where our patient lay
lifeless on the table,
a pond of warm blood
pooled beneath
the surgeon's feet,

and they forgot to describe
the way he would track
his wet red footprints
down the long corridor
towards the waiting room,

where the patient's family
would be lounging deliriously
in pleather recliners,
their sunken eyes
still full of hope.

Hands

We go to bed, bodies separate
but hands touching softly
and just at the fingertips.

When I wake in the morning
I wonder if we parted
only in dream.

Do you remember the night
we parked in your convertible
by the San Antonio river?

Our hands touched then,
our hands and nothing more,
palms warm and flush,

fingers interwoven
like the teeth of a zipper
locked in place.

When you were a boy
your father said you had the
hands of a surgeon,

firm but delicate, sensitive
to the faintest movements, outward
extensions of an inner pulse.

During our first year of marriage
you brought home thick rolls
of medical tape to practice on—

your hands weaving suture
as fine as strands of hair
along the outer rim,

tying meticulous knots
into one continuous ring
until you had memorized

the rhythm of each incision,
the push and pull
of two parts becoming one.

We each have a way
to locate ourselves in
this immense world,

an animal instinct
that shows us how to survive
in ways we were never taught.

You navigate your life
through touch,
through the feel of it,

needle and thread
sewing flesh
to soft flesh,

your hands
reaching for mine
in the dark.

Convergence

The painting has a life of its own.
I try to let it come through.   –Jackson Pollock

Sometimes after a long shift
I wander through the ICU

like I'm wandering through
a museum,

each patient displayed
through glass walls

like a work of art that
stops you with sadness.

Today I lingered at a scene
like the Pollock painting—

our patient from this morning
crashing like a mural

of chaos, the staff moving
around the bed

like the four corners
of a canvas—

medication dripping, blood
viscous as paint

splattering, the surgeon
re-opening the chest

like an artist ripping open
a new reality—

one in which a heart
doesn't drown

and the body's cracks
can be restored by brushstrokes

and the hues of beauty and suffering
never have to mix.

Mild

While snow blows around the rest
of the northern country,
we make our bed in morning fog
that seeps in silently
from the San Francisco Bay.

Here the air rarely dips
below freezing and the fruit
that grows along the Russian River
yields juice that speaks to the
tongue in understatements.

Here the tree petals blossom
in subtle pinks as early as
February and the transition
from winter to spring
is so effortless,

the way your fingertips
unfastened the silk buttons
of my wedding gown, one by one,
until my bare skin bloomed,
ready to start life all over again.

Part of Me

Looking at
the exposed heart
satiates something
inside of me

the part of me
that feels hungry
all the time

the part of me
that knows how much
the heart
and the tongue
have in common

the part of me
that realizes hunger
is just another word
for desire and desire
is just another word
for pain

and we all know
that pain is the greatest
motivator

which is why I wake
at 5am and drive
to the city to see
a chest cut open
the skin pulled back

because I'm afraid
that seeing a heart
this way
is the only way
I can see myself.

Anniversary

Nine years ago, I walked down
the aisle, parted from my father,
grafted to your side. The pastor
commented on our rings,
how they formed a perfect circle,
the shape of love, of unity,

but I wonder if love
is more like an empty room,
quiet and dark
like the chamber of a heart:

it allows itself
to be filled.

The blood returns to it thick
and blue, nothing to offer
but sheer volume.
When its walls are stretched
to capacity, it pumps the blood
back out, back to the lungs
so the whole body
can breathe again.

A circle, yes,
but more than a shape,
love is a rhythm—

the heart beating
the blood,
the blood feeding
the body,
a house and the ruins
it was built upon.

Compressions

As I perform my skills test
        on the rubber mannequin

it strikes me that
        the movements used

to save a life
        are the same repetitions

that create it—
        my hands lightly lifting

the chin as if I might kiss
        the cheek, my eyes

watching for rise and fall
        of the chest, my fingertips

placed at the vulnerable
        curve of the neck, feeling

for a pulse. And then
        my palms, one on top of

the other like two lovers' hips
        compressed, my fingers

intertwined like legs woven
        between sheets, pumping

my weight into the
        dummy's breastbone

with enough depth to squeeze
        the heart, enough thrust

to snap a rib, the way I imagine
        God did when He took

the shard of bone from Adam's side
     to form the woman—

the way their bodies swayed together
     for the first time,

her womb quivering
     like a heart starved for blood.

Pursuit

The air of our marriage has grown stale,
the way a house feels when you leave for a time
and come home again to find coffee cups
left in the sink, soaking in cold water, crumbs
from a hurried breakfast fallen to the floor,
the bed still unmade.

Or perhaps we're more like a fire that needs stoking—
if that is not too tired an analogy—with the logs
that once burned wild now wilting and graying,
the blind heat of the coals chipping and falling
to the uneven brick floor.

You always liked the spark, the raging flames,
the squeal and hiss of the wood surrendering,
but I was the one with the slow burn, the slow pulse
of flames contained inside of each ember, the possibility
of a reawakening always at the cusp, always at the mercy
of your steady, relentless breath.

Distance

Driving to work, I am thankful
for every dark mile, leaving behind
the dishes soaking in the sink,
the crumpled laundry abandoned
in baskets at the foot of the stairs,
the children still quiet under
the soft hood of sleep. This morning

I notice the street lights that line
the interstate in reliable intervals
like cordial encounters between people,
like the defined distance between
home and work. This morning

I want more than cordial. I'm running late
and am forced to park on the top deck
of the garage. My consolation prize
is the view from the roof—

cargo liners docked at the mouth
of the silver river and the tips
of old stone churches at my eye line.

Stepping out of my car, the sky
is spitting and the wind is trying
to wash something from me.

Today at the hospital,
looking down at an open chest
held apart by a steel retractor,
watching the taut knot
of ripe human muscle
pant like a hungry dog's lips—

I think I'm getting closer.

Absence

You forgot to turn off your alarm
        before you left. It wakes me at 6:30.

My arm reaches for your side of the bed.
        Empty. Even your pillow is gone.

I lie on my back and listen to the familiar
        wake-up repertoire of alarm clock songs

as the subtle sun of dawn sifts through
        the blinds like background music.

You like songs with gentle victories,
        the way you hum while doing the dishes,

the way you whistle along to old tunes
        you never tire of. I trace the sunken

space your body has made on the mattress
        over the past twelve years. Even absence

has a face. I stroke it with my fingertips.
        How much more we are than just bodies.

Even without you, I still feel you. I feel you
        the way I feel the music, and perhaps

that is all the spirit is anyway—a recognizable song
        that lingers long after the person is removed,

like the good part of a dream you revisit
        in your mind all day before it finally vanishes.

Midlife

It's always afternoon.

Our conversations
have become the white noise
of shallow waves
lapping at the shore.

The sand occasionally sighs
to let the ocean know
it's still listening

and the children
have been carried away
by the current—

look at them at the horizon
like fruit flies swarming
around a rim of warm vinegar.

The seagulls have snagged
the last crusts
of peanut butter sandwiches
wrapped in aluminum foil—

foil on sand, fire on earth,
the thunder rolls closer
and lightning remains
an unkept promise.

Our path home is a full moon
made of asphalt and fireflies.

Crows perch on
one-way street signs
and ambition stiffens
on the side of the road

as we take another turn
around this worn-out world.

The Meaning of Life

It is here—somewhere
in this old pancake shop
at the corner of 34th and Atlantic—
or so I tell myself
this Sunday morning,
early October, all five of us
shuffling in with our nice clothes,
bad breath, and gnawing
church-hunger.

Outside the tides are swelling,
waves slapping the ledge
of the boardwalk, wind
pressing so hard against the
restaurant doors that
customers can't get out.

It feels like a sad defeat
to accept it is not out there—
somewhere at the rugged slice
of horizon where cargo ships
come and go freely—

but it is here, too,
in this warm sticky room
full of people just rolled out of bed,
or never went to bed, dark circles
under our eyes as we look
at each other across glasses of
ice water and orange juice.

Perhaps this is life's greatest trick—
like the moment Dorothy is told
that all along she could have
clicked her own heels to get home.

This is the moment I must learn
to wake up at my own table.

Meanwhile, the food comes.
The waitress returns with her
burnt pot of coffee, not asking
if we want more, just filling.
I slice the children's stacks
into small square bites
and build a dam to block
the too-much-butter from engulfing
the entire plate. Sugar packets
litter the table top like confetti,
a game the kids play to pass
the time. Before the pancakes
have uncurled in their small,
ravenous stomachs, they have slithered
out of their chairs, hands deep
in the plastic jar of Dum-Dums
at the checkout counter. They fight
over who gets the cotton candy flavor.

Left behind are the pops with the
mystery wrappers, their dark maroon
question marks never answered.

Fall

Early November and the first
cold of the season. I've been
coughing all week, my sore lungs
bitten by the sharp autumn air
the same way that skin blisters
in the heavy light of summer.
My daughter lies in small
heap next to me on the old
slipcovered sofa. I watch her
muscles twitch under a restless
hedge of sleep, her body
tightened and finally flattened
by the violent throes of the
stomach flu. Outside the
living room window, the solitary
oak tree in our neighbor's yard
looks as though it's been dipped
head-first into a can of crimson paint,
red on top but still green on the
bottom, and I wonder why the
body is slower to adapt to the
weight of change, why the
heart is slower to comprehend
what the head has known for
so long, and why, like the leaves,
so much must happen before
we are ready to fall from
the branches that bore us,
to trust the air that slowly
carries us down.

Transplant

After the surgeon digs
the dying heart
out of our patient's chest,

he places it in a steel bowl
on the back table.

I lift the heart out of the bowl,
rest it in my cupped palms,
feeling the same way I feel
when I hold a newborn baby,
realizing it was just alive
inside another's body.

I am dumb and humbled—
all of the metaphors
now so obvious:

The human heart
is the poem.

This organ
is what the whole of life
is trying to say—

that in sickness
we enlarge and harden,
that the strongest of us
somehow remain
soft and supple—
pliable cores of
muscle and spark,

moving to an impulse
apart from logic.

We unwrap the donor heart
from the cooler of ice,
just flown in
from another state,
once housed by a man
who took his life
with a gunshot to the head.

The surgeon inspects
the new heart's anatomy,
sews it into the
carved-out cavity
of our patient's body.

When the cross-clamp is removed,
when the blood begins to flow,
the new heart beats again
in a body other than its own,

without a prompt,
without a shock,
without a word or whisper.

The surgeon looks up
from his work, says,

"Well, if this doesn't just amaze you,
you might as well be dead."

Cold Hope

After a cold front
the black birds return,

flying in thick swarms
from yard to yard,
stopping for a moment
to pick grain in the grass,

then off again
through a blue spotted sky
to perch and sing at the top
of tree skeletons.

When one rises
the whole group follows,
when they spread
their wings to fly
they reveal bright stripes
of red and gold.

It's like some kind of
January conspiracy,

the way they disappear
for days, running off
with the sun, arriving
again on my front lawn
like prodigal children
coming home.

Over time, we learn to take
what we can get. We swallow
it down and call it gratitude.

The senses dull. The only song
left to sing is the silent one
that rings deep in our bones:

Who do you think you are?

Shut the doors and lock them.
Keep out the cold. Burrow
into the dark crevices of your
own making.

Try as you might, light
finds a way in—

through the walls,
through the windows,
squawking like blackbirds
with beaks raised,

praising the unspoken
pulses we don't understand
but long to be part of.

Sustenance

Life is pain
but we also know
it is sweet and
worth holding onto,

so we cling to
the little things—

the bag of coffee ground to
fine dust, measured out
in spoonfuls at the same time
each morning,

the dog's paws pacing
in and out of the bedroom,
beckoning for breakfast,
nails clacking on wooden
floors like a clock ticking
in the back of my mind,
rousing me from dream,
from that place where time
and hunger don't exist.

This morning,
the first day of February,
the sun has risen again
and without my doing.

I wake to feed the dog,
feed the children, put away
the dishes we ate from last night.
I prepare sandwiches wrapped
tightly in tin foil, pack them in
plastic lunch bags for later,
add a piece of fruit for each child—
mandarin oranges today—

which they will hold
like small globes in the
center of their hands,
peeling them apart
one wedge at a time,
the bitter pith burrowing
beneath their fingernails,
the sweet juice filling
their eager mouths.

Outside the window
mist rises from the frozen lawn.
Frost-covered branches thaw
in the warmth of dawn,
beads of water dripping
to the ground where
fallen leaves dissolve
back into the earth that
bore them.

March

This morning the distant
sound

of a leaf blower
jolts me

from a resigned winter
slumber.

How dare he! I curse
my neighbor

and his revving motor,
ridding

the flower beds of last year's
leaves.

The sun, too, is on the run,
winding

the final curve of its orbit,
rising earlier,

staying out later. But wait—the sun
doesn't move—

it hangs unwavering in the black
blanket of space!

We are the sphere in constant
rotation,

caught in our constant craving
for light.

Do you feel it? The vacillation
of the earth,

always spinning yet never
arriving

like a revolving door
with no exit,

like a man fleeing the stories
of his past

only to relive them again
and again.

Negligence

What happens when we
care for the hearts of others
is two things:

We become better.
And our world falls apart.

Please tell me
there's something
ugly on the outside
that still has a good
chance at life.
Remind me of the things
that grow despite me,
in spite of me.

When my first child
was an infant, I left her
with another to return to work.
Every day I was amazed
she survived without me.
And now, my daughters
with their wild, tangled
hair and mismatched
clothes go into their world
and have themselves
a promising day.

This morning, I realize
it's as simple as the birds
hitching a ride on a big
March wind, blowing in
from a place I cannot see.
It's as simple as the robin
perching his warm copper chest
on tree outside my window.

God, the tree looks hideous
right now: gray, brittle, dull.

But think of what's inside of it—
petals, hidden color, deep roots.

It's about to break open.

Note to Self

The desk still holds my red elbows.
My hands still cup my face
as I gaze through tired windows.
My knees still bend. The chair
still supports my heavy longings.

There are still voices
that string up my heart
and tug it along by a
piece of twine until it's
outside my own body.

>Here they tell it to beat again,
>here they tell it to beat for them.

But the twine has begun to
unravel. I watch each thread
twist apart until my fingers
can feel the frayed endings,
the rough edges that mark
a true separation.

There is this and only this.
Stop staring at the horizon.
Life exists where it's always been,

>In the soft billows inside of me.
>In the soft rhythms inside of me.

Exhale

Last night, the violet vein of the sky
        let go. All of this volume
had to feed something. In the morning,
        we wake to a birth.

I watch from the window as my children
        cut the first footprints into the
unsullied surface of snow. The day
        grows like an infant.

The shadows of tree limbs switch positions
        upon the white lawn as the sun
pushes its way across the sky.
        I imagine my current self—

the gray strands sprouting at my hairline,
        the crevices under my eyes settling
in deep angles like afternoon light,
        a different kind of birth.

My tongue has grown tired. My husband builds a fire.
        I listen to the flames quietly ramble on
like an old woman talking about time
        as she slowly exhales.

Libby Kurz holds a BS in Nursing from UNC-Charlotte and an MFA in Creative Writing from National University. Her work has been published in *The Poet's Billow, Relief Journal, Driftwood Press, Literary Mama, Ruminate, The Hunger,* and *Mothers Always Write.* Her poetry was awarded first prize in the New Voices category of the Poetry Society of Virginia's 2017 Contest. She is an assistant editor and regular contributor at *Red Tent Living,* an online faith-based publication for women. A veteran of the US Air Force, she now resides on the coast of Virginia with her family. When she's not keeping tabs on her three kids, she works as registered nurse in the operating room and teaches creative writing workshops online and at The Muse Writers Center in Norfolk, VA. She is passionate about a good cup of coffee, bumming on the beach, and finding meaning in the ordinary moments of life. https://libbykurz.com.

www.ingramcontent.com/pod-product-compliance
Lightning Source LLC
LaVergne TN
LVHW051609080426
835510LV00020B/3213